→ KNOW YOUR ←

PIGS

JACK BYARD

Know Your Pigs © Jack Byard, 2009, 2012
All rights reserved.

First published in Great Britain in 2009 by Old Pond Publishing Ltd.
First published in North America in 2011 by Fox Chapel Publishing, 1970 Broad Street, East
Petersburg, PA 17520, USA. Published under license.

ISBN: 978-1-56523-611-0

Library of Congress Cataloging-in-Publication Data

Byard, Jack.
    Know your pigs / Jack Byard. -- 1st ed.
        p. cm.
    "First published in Great Britain in 2009 by Old Pond Publishing Ltd."--T.p. verso.
    ISBN 978-1-56523-611-0
    1. Swine as pets. 2. Swine breeds. I. Title.
SF395.6.B93 2011
636.4--dc22
                                        2011017571

To learn more about the other great books from Fox Chapel Publishing, or to find a retailer near you,
call toll-free 800-457-9112 or visit us at www.FoxChapelPublishing.com.

Note to Authors: We are always looking for talented authors to write new books. Please send a brief
letter describing your idea to Acquisition Editor, 1970 Broad Street, East Petersburg, PA 17520.

Printed in China
First printing

CONTENTS

Pig Talk

SOW: A female pig.

BOAR: A male pig.

PIGLET: A baby pig of eight weeks old or less.

GILT: A young sow.

LITTER: The brood of young born to a pig.

SHOAT: A young pig that has just been weaned.

FARROW: A litter of piglets.

HOG/SWINE: Other terms for pig.

LANDRACE: A domesticated animal adapted to t[h]e natural environment in which it lives.

FOREWORD

Pigs, hogs or swine, whatever you call them, have been around man for 11,000 years. Over these years they have provided us with food and, in earlier times, bones for tools and weapons, skin for shields and bristles for brushes.

Pigs are considered to have intelligence beyond that of a human three year old. In the last few years numbers of this bright-eyed animal have declined dramatically and a number of breeds have become extinct.

Whose fault is it? The government, the environment and food fashions must, to my mind, all take some of the blame. Often, I feel, rules and regulations are created by people who know little about the industry and on occasions care even

less. We should not discard breeds because they are currently unfashionable or do not fit in with the modern way of life.

Rare breeds societies and dedicated breeders do what they can to protect endangered species but we must all help to preserve the rare and endangered animals on this fragile earth. As the T-shirt slogan tells us, extinction is forever.

Jack Byard

Bradford, 2011

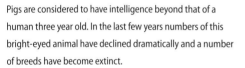

AMERICAN GUINEA HOG

....

NATIVE TO
USA

NOW FOUND
In small numbers in the USA

Loves a good tummy rub
and back scratch

Usually black but occasionally with a reddish tint, American Guinea Hogs have upright ears, a hairy coat and a curly tail.

The American Guinea Hog is a critically rare breed of pig that is unique to the USA. The original pigs were imported from the Canary Islands and West Africa in the seventeenth century.

The original Guinea Hog was crossed with several other breeds. Because these are now extinct, it is impossible to create a complete and accurate picture of the true history of the breed. One possible contributing breed is the small black Essex pig, also extinct, which is known to have lived in southeastern USA where most Guinea hogs are to be found.

The American Guinea Hog once foraged for its own food and ate roots, grass, nuts, rodents and even snakes. The breed is now kept on small farms and large ranches where they will keep the area clear of vermin. Their friendly, docile nature is an added bonus. This hardy little pig loves a good tummy rub and back scratch. It cannot be allowed to become extinct.

AMERICAN LANDRACE

....

NATIVE TO
USA

NOW FOUND
USA

Noted for
excellent quality pork

Coming in any color—as long as it is white—the American Landrace has long drooping ears and a long muscular body covered in fine hair.

The American Landrace is a descendant of the Danish Landrace, which originated at the end of the nineteenth century. The Danish Landrace is itself descended from the crossing of the Yorkshire with native Danish breeds.

In the 1930s, the Danish and United States governments agreed Danish Landrace hogs could be imported into the United States on the understanding they would not be used for commercial breeding. In the following years, comparisons between the Danish Landrace and the American native breeds were carried out and when breeding restrictions were lifted in the 1950s, the years of research paid off. The Danish Landrace hogs were crossed with China Whites and Landrace hogs imported from Norway and Sweden, the first step in producing the modern fast-growing, sturdy American Landrace. The breed is noted for its usefulness in crosses with other breeds and its excellent quality pork. It is also used in medical research to test human vaccines.

BENTHEIM BLACK PIED

NATIVE TO
Lower Saxony in Germany

NOW FOUND
Europe

White with black spots in grey rings

The Bentheim Black Pied is white with black spots in grey rings and has lopped ears.

The Bentheim Black Pied or Buntes Bentheimer Schwein originated at the beginning of the twentieth century and was named after the district in Lower Saxony where it was first bred. It is a cross between local breeds of pigs and the Berkshire. The Bentheim Black Pied was bred in the area until the late-1950s when tastes changed and demand for it declined. Extinction loomed.

The herd book was closed in 1964. One breeder kept meticulous records and the book was reopened in 1988 but numbers continued to decline. Animal breeding regulations within Germany created further obstacles; each area would have its own breed association, which was not an ideal situation for a breed at risk. In 2003, the Association for the Conservation of the Bentheim Black Pied Pig came into being and things started to look brighter. The herd books were merged, the population of animals rose from 50 to 420 and registered breeders from 19 to 90 over four years.

BERSHIRE

NATIVE TO
British Isles

NOW FOUND
North America, Australia and New Zealand

The oldest breed in Britain—discovered by Oliver Cromwell

The Berkshire is black with prick ears, white socks and a white tip to the tail and a white flash on the face.

Oliver Cromwell and his troops discovered the Berkshire pig while in winter quarters near Reading in England. It is reputed to be the oldest breed in Britain and is noted for its size and color.

It is recorded that the first Berkshires were imported into America in 1823 and were crossed with the local breeds, which were improved in quality and size. Eventually there was not a purebred Berkshire to be found. In 1875, a boar by the grand name of Windsor Castle was imported. In the same year, a group of American importers and breeders met to discuss how to ensure the breed remained pure and the American Berkshire Association was formed. The first boar to be recorded was the Ace of Spades from a herd bred by Queen Victoria of England.

It is said the Berkshire is at its best being cared for with good housing and food but in New Zealand, it wanders freely and is inclined to graze.

BLACK IBERIAN/ SPANISH

NATIVE TO
Iberian Peninsula

NOW FOUND
Portugal and Spain

Diet of acorns gives
ham unique flavor

The Black Iberian is completely black, including its hooves.

The Iberian pig is specific to the Mediterranean and is the last known breed to live entirely in the open, mainly under the cover of oak trees growing in Andalusia and the mountains of Spain. The microclimate of the area is ideal for the oak tree's growth and consequently for the acorns, the main food of the Black Iberian. This diet helps to give the ham its unique flavor. The production is for quality not quantity.

The Iberian pig is rare but well regulated, only 15 pigs per 2.5 acres are allowed. The Iberian pig has a special place in the pig world: by sheer quality, it has defied economics and the fickle public for centuries.

BRITISH SADDLEBACK

NATIVE TO
England

NOW FOUND
British Isles, Nigeria and the Seychelles

Good starter pig
for small farmers

The British Saddleback is black apart from an unbroken white band over the shoulders and down to the front feet.

Two English pig breeds, the Wessex Saddleback from the Isle of Purbeck and the Essex from East Anglia, were first recognized in herd books in 1918. The Essex was a finer, lighter pig with four white socks and a broad saddle; it was known as the "gentleman's pig." The Wessex had only two white socks at the front and was known as the Farmer's Choice. The breeds were combined in 1967 and jointly called the British Saddleback.

The British Saddleback is a hardy, docile animal and because its skin color protects it from sunburn, it is well suited to outdoor conditions. It is considered a good starter pig for small farmers, thanks to its good temperament. The lop-eared animals are considered more manageable than the prick-eared ones. As for the flavor and succulence of the Saddleback bacon, experts have classed it as "mouth-watering."

CHESTER WHITE

NATIVE TO
Pennsylvania, USA

NOW FOUND
North America

Developed from semi-wild hogs in Pennsylvania

The Chester White is all white with droopy ears.

In the eighteenth century, most hogs in Pennsylvania were semi-wild and foraged in the woodlands for beechnuts and hazelnuts. They were far from docile and did not produce quality meat.

In the nineteenth century, a Captain Jeffries decided it was time to tame these animals. He imported a boar from England, either a Cumberland (now extinct) or a breed from Bedfordshire, and crossed it with his white sows to develop the Chester County White. The breed became very popular and Captain Jefferies was soon selling the offspring to local farmers and hiring out his boar.

The hogs were fed on fruit, grain and vegetables and the diet produced animals that were docile and fast growing. They weighed up to twice as much as their semi-wild ancestors and produced quality meat. Further developments used the Yorkshire and breeds from Lincolnshire in England to create the Chester White we know today. It is now the sixth most popular hog breed in America and a producer of lean quality meat.

CHOCTAW HOG

NATIVE TO
USA

NOW FOUND
Mainly in the Choctaw Nation of Oklahoma

Runs free, foraging for roots,
acorns, berries and plants

The Choctaw is usually black but occasionally has white markings.

This pig is traditionally kept by the Choctaw Native Americans. The Choctaw Hog descends from pigs brought to America by Spaniards in the sixteenth century but later were bred by Native Americans in the southeastern states. When the Choctaw people moved from the Deep South to Oklahoma, they took these pigs with them. Today's hogs are the direct descendants of the Oklahoma stock and their appearance has not changed in more than 150 years.

The hogs are still reared in the traditional manner. They are earmarked and then released to run free, foraging for roots, acorns, berries and plants. They are periodically rounded up and sorted for market, breeding or meat and those that are released hurtle back into the woodland with surprising agility.

The Choctaw Hog is critically rare but does not have a high profile within the food industry. As a result, the money needed to preserve this part of American history has so far been slow in coming.

DUROC

NATIVE TO
USA

NOW FOUND
North America and on most continents

Named after the breeder's prize stallion

The Duroc is golden brown to rich red mahogany.

The Duroc is one of America's oldest breeds. In 1812, pigs known as Red Hogs were bred in New York and New Jersey. In 1823, Isaac Frink of Saratoga bought, from Harry Kelsey, a red boar he named after Kelsey's prize stallion, Duroc. Kelsey claimed the boar had been imported but writers of porcine history, after much research, are unable to say for sure. By the mid-nineteenth century, systematic crossing of the red boar's descendants with the Red Hogs produced the modern Duroc. At the Chicago World's Fair in 1893, the first successful Duroc Hog Show was held and it helped to establish the reputation of this beautiful animal.

Their thick coat enables them to survive cold winters but the coat molts in summer allowing the Duroc to cope with hot weather. Because of their coloring, they are less prone to sunburn. Their excellent meat is sweet, tender and juicy with a mild flavor.

GLAMROCK

....

NATIVE TO
England

NOW FOUND
England and North America

No litter has two
identical piglets

The Glamrock is black, white and ginger with spots and speckles.

As a result of feedback from their customers, English pig breeders Simon and Sarah Righton decided to produce a breed that retained the intense flavor of their Gloucestershire Old Spots while being more acceptable for the modern health-conscious market.

The boar chosen for this task was a Hamroc, itself a cross between the Duroc and the Hampshire. The color variations of the piglets were no great surprise; no litter has two identical piglets and combines the spots of the Gloucestershire Old Spots sow, the black and white of the Hampshire and the ginger of the Duroc.

GLOUCESTERSHIRE OLD SPOTS

....

NATIVE TO
England

NOW FOUND
North America and most continents

Hardy and can spend
the year outdoors

Gloucestershire Old Spots have a white coat with clearly defined black spots and large floppy ears that cover their faces down to the snout.

The Gloucestershire Old Spots is the oldest pedigreed spotted pig breed in the world.

It appears to be the result of crossing the original Gloucester with the unimproved Berkshire, a sandy-colored pig with spots. The Gloucestershire Old Spots must have at least one spot. The fashion has changed over the years from very spotty pigs to ones where it was hard to find the single spot and back again.

The large docile Gloucestershire Old Spots is very hardy and, provided they have warm and dry shelter, they can happily spend the entire year outdoors. They once grazed orchards eating the windfall apples to supplement their diet. Indeed, Gloucestershire folklore has it that the spots are bruises from the falling fruit. Also known also as the Gloster Spot, Old Spot, The Cottager's Pig and The Orchard Pig.

HAMPSHIRE

NATIVE TO
USA

NOW FOUND
Worldwide

Oldest and leanest
American breed

The Hampshire is a black pig with a white belt. The belt is a strip of white across the shoulders and around the body covering the front legs. The ears are erect.

The Hampshire is thought to be the oldest early American breed in existence. The original breeding pigs were Wessex or Wessex Saddleback crosses exported to America between 1825 and 1835 from a farm in Hampshire in the British Isles. The original American name was The Thin Rind but the breed was renamed the Hampshire in 1890.

The Hampshire became very popular worldwide. In just one year during the 1970s, more than 600 pigs were exported to 14 countries. In the world of pig breeding, the Hampshire has found its place. With a reputation as the leanest of the North American breeds, it produces quality pork and bacon. In many countries, the Hampshire is used extensively as a sire for crossbred pigs.

HEREFORD

....

NATIVE TO
USA

NOW FOUND
USA

Unique American breed,
docile and adaptable

The Herford's color varies from dark to light reddish-brown but deep red is preferred. The face is mainly white and slightly dished. They have medium-sized droopy ears and at least two white feet.

The Hereford hog is a unique American breed with, to my knowledge, no connection with Hereford in England. The first Hereford hogs are credited to Mr. R. U. Webber of La Plata, Missouri, who in 1902 crossed the Duroc, Chester White and the Ohio Improved Chester. Unfortunately, administrative issues mean that the modern Hereford cannot be traced back to this line.

From 1920 to 1925, a group of breeders established a breed also called the Hereford. This was a cross of the Duroc, the Poland White and possibly a twist of Chester White and Hampshire. In 1934, 100 animals were chosen as foundation stock and the National Hereford Hog Record was established in the same year.

The Hereford is docile and able to adapt to indoor or outdoor breeding and variations in climate. They make an ideal choice for a small-scale breeder and produce superb meat.

KUNE KUNE

NATIVE TO
New Zealand

NOW FOUND
USA and Europe

The name is Maori
for fat and round

The Kune Kune's color varies between ginger, brown, black, cream and spotted. They usually have a pair of tassels called Piri Piri under the chin.

Kune Kune (pronounced kooney kooney—Maori for fat and round) pigs are from New Zealand but their true country of origin is in doubt. It is possible the Maoris took them there because similar breeds can be found in Polynesia. Whalers from various countries released pigs on the islands to produce a food source for later visits. The pigs that came with Captain Cook on his first voyage to the island may also have contributed to the Kune Kune. The breed, also known as the Maori Pig, was brought to the USA in 1995.

The Kune Kune is a delightful looking little pig with short legs and a short round body. They are 23 to 26 inches tall and can weigh from 139 to 240 pounds. They are placid, easy to keep and enjoy human company. The Kune Kune feeds mainly on grass so are good lawn mowers, and they produce excellent pork.

LACOMBE

....

NATIVE TO
Canada

NOW FOUND
North America, Mexico, Japan, Russia,
Puerto Rico and Italy

Developed in Alberta but now rare

Lacombe are all white with droopy ears.

The Lacombe was developed at the Agriculture Canada Research Station in Lacombe, Alberta. It is a cross of the Canadian Landrace, the Berkshire and the Chester White. The Lacombe was created and developed over many years by John Gilmore Stothart and Howard Fredeen, who brought their extensive scientific knowledge to the task. The Lacombe was slightly heavier and fatter than the Landrace and when it appeared in the market in 1957, it put Lacombe on the international scientific map. By 1981, the Lacombe was the fifth most popular hog in Canada with just under 2,000 animals registered.

Unfortunately, the Lacombe is not as popular now as it was in its early days and, as with many other hogs in Canada, numbers are falling dramatically. At the last count in 2009, there were only 200 of this gentle breed remaining. Its situation is classed as critical by Rare Breeds Canada.

LARGE BLACK

....

NATIVE TO
England

NOW FOUND
North America, British Isles and New Zealand

Excellent mothers able to raise large litters

Large Blacks are always black.

The Large Black is Britain's only all-black pig. It originates from the Old English Hog in the sixteenth and seventeenth centuries. In the late-nineteenth century, there were two types of Large Black, one in Devon and Cornwall and another in East Anglia. The Large Black Society brought the two types together in 1889.

The Large Black is found throughout the country and kept in small herds, some of which were established early in the twentieth century. In the 1960s, a trend toward intensive rearing led to a decline in the breed because it was unsuitable for this type of farming. Extremely docile and hardy, it is ideally suited to simple outdoor rearing systems. This characteristic and its color made it popular for overseas breeding and by 1935 it had been exported to more than 30 countries.

Large Black sows are excellent mothers able to bring up large litters with just basic food. They once grazed orchards eating the windfall fruit and being fed whey. The Large Black produces superb quality meat.

MANGALITSA

NATIVE TO
Hungary and Austria

NOW FOUND
North America and Europe

An ancient pig with curly wool that can survive harsh winters

Mangalitsa can be Swallow Bellied, black with a white belly; Blonde, grey to yellow; or Red, a color similar to the Tamworth.

The Mangalitsa is an ancient pig with curly wool. In the early part of the twentieth century, it was crossed with the Lincolnshire Curly Coat, which had been exported to Hungary and Austria. The Lincolnshire Curly Coat became extinct in 1972.

Mangalitsa meat products were at one time in great demand all over Europe and were traded on the Vienna Stock Exchange. The breed was famed for its hardiness, due in part, to the woolly curly coat, which provides superb insulation. The Mangalitsa is able to survive the harshest winters and long hot summers without the problems of sunburn.

Heath Putnam introduced the Mangalitsa to America in 2007. He had spent years working in Europe and decided this quality product would be appreciated by America's discerning consumers. Traditionally, the meat is used for salami and Parma Ham because of its superb flavor.

MEIDAM

NATIVE TO
British Isles

NOW FOUND
Worldwide

Grows fast, producing
excellent lean meat

The Meidam is white with pink skin and semi-lop ears. It is physically similar to a Landrace but slightly shorter.

The Meidam (pronounced Maydam) is a modern breed, accepted and registered at the beginning of the twenty-first century. Its genetic make-up is approximately one-fourth Meishan, one-fourth Large White and one-half British Landrace. The goal was to capture the advantages of the Meishan sow, which are larger litter sizes and excellent mothering ability, and retain the European breeds' benefits of growth rate and excellent lean meat.

So the Meidam is a "synthetic" breed, created with a commercial purpose, but using the genes of long-established pure breeds.

This was not the first time that Chinese pig genes have been used to create a "native" British breed. It is thought that imported Chinese pigs also contributed to the Yorkshire in the 1800s.

MEISHAN

....

NATIVE TO
China

NOW FOUND
In small numbers on most continents

Floppy ears cover its eyes

The Meishan is black with heavily wrinkled face and skin. Their flop ears cover their eyes.

The Meishan (pronounced Mayshawn) comes from a narrow belt of land between north and central China in the lower Changjiang river basin. It is an area of lakes and valleys with a mild climate. The pigs are well fed on farm by-products, water plants and concentrates. The Meishan is fat and slow growing but has excellently flavored meat.

The breed was first imported into America in 1989. The Meishan is relatively disease resistant, docile and an extremely good mother. It is usually crossed with the Yorkshire to produce excellent quality meat.

MIDDLE WHITE

NATIVE TO
England

NOW FOUND
Worldwide

Succulent meat is darker
than most pork

The Middle White has a thick white coat, snub nose, dished face and large pricked-up ears.

The Middle White was first recognized in 1852 at an agricultural show in Keighley, West Yorkshire. At the show, Joseph Tulley exhibited the Middle Whites alongside the Large Whites and Small Whites. The judges agreed about the fine quality of the breed but felt they were too small for Large Whites and too large for Small Whites and so a third class for the Middle White was born. It is now the smallest British pig; the Small White became extinct in 1912.

Crossing local breeds with Chinese and Siamese pigs from which the Middle White inherits its characteristic dished face created the breed.

The succulent meat of the Middle White is much darker than that of other breeds and is in great demand in Japan, where it is known as the Middle Yorks. It is said to be the only pork the Emperor will eat. In 1990, the Middle White Pig Breeders Club was created yet, despite this increased interest, this is still a breed more rare than the Giant Panda.

MULEFOOT

. . . .

NATIVE TO
USA

NOW FOUND
USA

Has a one-piece hoof,
not cloven or divided

The Mulefoot has mainly a black soft hair coat with medium floppy ears and a single hoof. The Mulefoot, as its name implies, has a one-piece hoof (not cloven or divided like other hog breeds) and is the only mule footed breed of pig to have a breed standard.

The National Mulefoot Hog Breeders Association began in 1908 and within 2 years, further registers were opened to include 235 breeders across 22 states. Today, however, the Mulefoot has the unenviable record of being the rarest hog breed in America with less than 200 being registered annually.

In 1964, a Louisiana breeder named Holiday gathered all remaining Mulefoot hogs and for almost 40 years had the only ones in America. Through his sterling efforts, the breed was saved from extinction.

This hardy breed has a high resistance to many hog diseases and is being studied in the hope of finding a cure for lameness in their cloven-hoofed cousins. The Mulefoot produces quality rose-red colored tender meat that always comes out top in blind tastings.

OSSABAW ISLAND HOG

....

NATIVE TO
Ossabaw Island off the coast of Georgia, USA

NOW FOUND
On Ossabaw Island and a few in Georgia

Found only on islands off
the Georgia coast

Ossabaw Island Hogs are black, spotted black-and-white or red-and-tan. They have heavy coats, pricked-up ears and long snouts.

The Ossabaw Island pigs are a rare South American breed. They are descendants of the animals brought to this New World island by the Spaniards more than 450 years ago. In most environments, feral pigs will cross with domestic breeds but this is not the case on Ossabaw Island. They have developed and bred in total isolation.

In spring, food is in short supply so over the centuries the Ossabaw Island Hog has adapted to the food cycle with a method of storing fat to see them through the periods when food is scarce. Over time, they have also become smaller.

Because of quarantine restrictions, it is not possible to import the pigs directly from the island. The herds on the mainland today are descended from a group that left the island in 1970, before the restrictions. The meat is of superb quality with a fat profile high in Omega 3 and beautifully marbled with a rich wild flavor.

Oxford Sandy and Black

NATIVE TO
England

NOW FOUND
British Isles

Happiest foraging outdoors in woodland

They are pale to dark gold with black blotches - not spots. The ears are lopped or semi-lopped. The boar has a white tip to the tail, four white feet and ideally a white blaze.

The Oxford Sandy and Black has existed for more than 300 years and was a traditional cottager's pig around Oxfordshire. It is one of the oldest pig breeds in the British Isles. In the 1940s, the breed declined, and by 1985, extinction appeared inevitable. Were it not for the efforts of Steven Kimmins, Andrew J. Sheppey and Geoffrey Cloke, the Oxford and Sandy Black would be no more.

The main body color is due to its Tamworth ancestry. The Oxford Sandy and Black is also known as the Plum Porridge, the Plum Pudding and the Oxford Forest. The Oxford Sandy and Black is happiest outdoors foraging in woodland or rough grazing. Its color gives it great protection against sunburn and its long coat makes it tolerant of wet weather.

The Oxford Sandy and Black is an amiable animal to manage so is ideal for small farmers and produces meat of excellent quality and flavor.

POLAND CHINA

NATIVE TO
The Miami Valley, Butler and
Warren Counties, Ohio

NOW FOUND
USA and Cyprus

Large and able to travel

The Poland China is a large black pig with white patches.

The breed owes its origins to so many different breeds of pigs it is difficult to know where to start. In 1816, John Wallace bought four Big China Hogs, one boar and three sows. Two of the sows were white and the third had black spots. These Big China Hogs were popular in Virginia, Maryland, Pennsylvania and Kentucky. There is also evidence pointing to the bloodline of pigs bred by an English duke that have similar coloring and came from Kentucky about that time. Whatever their origins, the quality of meat is superb.

There were two important requirements when breeding a Poland China: it had to be large and it had to be able to travel. Pigs were driven to market and this frequently meant a journey of a hundred miles.

TAMWORTH

NATIVE TO
England

NOW FOUND
North America, British Isles, Australia
and New Zealand

Foraging helps to reclaim scrubland

Tamworths are a rich golden brown.

Originating in Staffordshire in the early nineteenth century, the Tamworth is possibly the purest of English native pigs. It is classed as being rather primitive because of its long snout—the longest of any modern breed—and pricked-up ears. Credit for its color is due to the introduction of a red boar from Ireland.

The Tamworth became well established and, thanks to its adaptability, by the end of the nineteenth century it was being exported to Australia, North America and South East Asia. Records from the early twentieth century show pigs similar to the Tamworth running wild in the Otago region of South Island, New Zealand.

The Tamworth is ideal for rearing in outdoor systems and is used for reclaiming wood and scrubland. It is the perfect four-legged plowing machine. In winter, they will quite happily live in a hut in a snow-covered field. Their golden brown color gives protection from sunburn, which is a serious problem for paler-colored breeds.

VIETNAMESE POT BELLIED

....

NATIVE TO
The Red River Delta in Vietnam

NOW FOUND
North America, Europe, the Middle East,
Indonesia, Japan and Vietnam

Good pet for large gardens and small farms

Vietnamese Pot Bellies are black with wrinkled skin, especially around the face. They have small upright ears, a hanging belly, short legs and a short straight tail.

There are approximately 2.5 million Vietnamese Pot Bellied pigs in Vietnam. They arrived in the USA and Europe in the 1960s and were popular with zoos and animal parks during the 1970s. In the 1980s, the idea of keeping a pig as a pet took off. In the USA in 1986, a pig cost several thousand dollars.

The original Vietnamese Pot Bellies were not ideal house pets but since then, the breed has been improved beyond belief and is now a good pet for those with a large garden or a small farm because they have an extremely good temperament. A modern fully-grown animal can weigh from 66 pounds to 220 pounds, and the male is the smaller of the two. Because the Vietnamese Pot Bellied has been crossed with many other breeds, it is considered impossible to find a purebred.

WELSH

NATIVE TO
Wales

NOW FOUND
British Isles and in small numbers
in USA and Canada

Gentle and fun to keep

The Welsh pig is white with lop ears meeting just short of the snout. The perfect Welsh pig is pear-shaped when viewed from above or either side.

Originally, the Welsh pig came to prominence in 1870 when large numbers were sold into Cheshire for fattening on milk by-products. The Welsh Pig Society was founded in 1920. The Old Glamorgan Pig Society represented breeds similar to the Welsh from the Cardigan, Pembroke and Carmarthen areas. The two societies amalgamated in 1922 to become the Welsh Pig Society.

The Welsh is a hardy breed and will thrive under most conditions, indoors or out. Little is written about their personalities apart from one breeder who says they are gentle and fun to keep.

The breed reached its peak in the British Isles in 1947 but is now at risk with less than 200 in Wales and 600 in the British Isles. Happily, today it is growing in popularity in the USA and can be found in California and North Carolina, as well as in Canada.

WILD HOG

NATIVE TO
USA and Europe

NOW FOUND
USA and Europe

The original razorback

There are three types of wild pig in the USA: the Wild Hog, the Feral Hog and a hybrid.

Wild Hogs are mainly black with stiff bristles along the back, which are raised when the hog is disturbed and earned it the nickname "razorback." They were imported into the USA in the late-nineteenth century and were released into forests and game reserves in order to be hunted for sport. It is believed these hogs came from the Ural Mountains of Russia. A dog hunt in a reserve in 1920 killed two hogs but scattered a great number into the mountainous countryside where their descendants live today.

Feral hogs have been in the southern states of America since the sixteenth century. Pigs were amongst the most common livestock and inevitably some domestic pigs escaped to live in the wild. Their descendants form today's feral hog population. Pigs that have gone feral tend to be much larger than their domestic counterparts but otherwise look similar.

Hybrid Wild Hogs are a cross between the other two. These animals tend to have longer snouts and legs and straight tails.

YORKSHIRE

NATIVE TO
USA

NOW FOUND
North America

Hardy and happy,
found in every state

Yorkshires are white with pink skin, erect ears and a slightly dished face.

A weaver called John Tulley developed the ancestors of the American Yorkshire in Yorkshire in the north of England.

The first Yorkshires were imported into Ohio in 1830 and were not an immediate success. It was almost 100 years before the potential and the quality of this breed were fully realized. Jess Andrew Sr. of West Point in Indiana imported several English Large White hogs, which are the English equivalent of the Yorkshire, and with a breeding program, produced a Yorkshire hog that was appropriate to the American farmer and became nationally accepted. Today they are found in nearly every state.

The Yorkshire was bred to be almost self-sufficient. It produces large litters and is happy spending its life foraging outdoors. It is hardy and able to withstand varying and extreme conditions. The Yorkshire produces excellent quality meat.

Acknowledgments

I must once again thank owners and breeders for their help in producing this book. Without their unflagging enthusiasm and willingness to answer questions, I would sit in front of a blank monitor. Thanks also to my granddaughter Rebecca, whose pithy comments spur me on to readable texts. Finally, thank you to Professor D. Phillip Sponenberg of the Virginia-Maryland Regional College of Veterinary Medicine for his help at the eleventh hour.

If there are mistakes, they are mine and mine alone.

Jack Byard
Bradford, 2011

Picture Credits

(1) Jim Perkins, (2) PEAK Swine Genetics Inc., (3) VEBBS e. V, (4) Debbie Kingsley, (5) IberGour.com, (6) Forthill Farm, (7) Yantis Farm, (8) Professor D Phillip Sponenberg, DVM, PHD, (9) "Dever Hover" 58 jan@wtms.biz, (10) Cotswold Farm Park, (11) Penner Hampshires Inc. John and Zella Penner, (12) William Morrow, (13) Hannah Smith, (14) Peak Swine Genetics, (15) www.oaklandpigs.co.uk, (16) Pig Paradise Farm, (17) Courtesy ACMC Ltd, (18) Courtesy ACMC Ltd, (19) www.oaklandpigs.co.uk, (20) Don Schrider-ALBC, (21) Emile DeFelice, (22) Yorkshire Meats, Angus Turnbull, (23) Dr. Esther Gallant, (24) Odds Farm Park, (25) Helen and Rob Rose, (26) The Welsh Pedigree Pig Society, Darren Davies, (27) Suwannee River Ranch, (28) John and Zella Penner, (New Breed) Simon and Sarah Righton.